D1413858

DESTINATION
ASTEROIDS, COMETS, AND METEORS

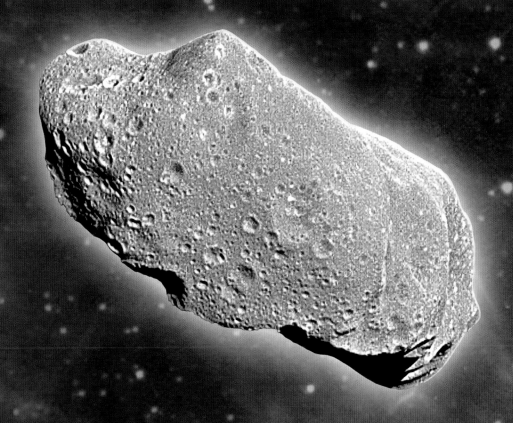

GILES SPARROW

PowerKiDS
press
New York

Published in 2010 by The Rosen Publishing Group
29 East 21st Street, New York, NY 10010

© 2010 The Brown Reference Group Ltd

U.S. Editor: Kara Murray

Picture Credits
Key: t – top, b – below, c – center, l – left, r – right. ESA: 15;
iStockphoto: Carmen Martinez Banus 21t, Clifford Mueller 16-17;
NASA: Don Davis 23b, 28, ESA 9t, GSFC 9b, 19, JHU/APL 13,
JPL TP, 2, 2-3, 8, 10t, 11b, 12-13, JPL-Caltech 6, 14-15;
Science Photo Library: 21b, Julian Baum 10b, ESA 16,
Tony & Daphne Hallas 24, Claus Lunau 18, NASA 23t,
David Parker 22; Shutterstock: Giovanni Benintende
5b, 20-21, David Gilder 26-27, Kevin H. Knuth 20,
Mozzyb 25t, Dmitry Pichugin 26l, Kenneth V. Pilon
5t, 27t; SIL: 11t; Source: 29

Front cover: NASA: bl, JPL (c); Back cover:
NASA: JPL; Backgrounds: NASA

Library of Congress Cataloging-in-Publication Data

Sparrow, Giles.
    Destination asteroids, comets, and meteors / Giles Sparrow. — 1st ed.
        p. cm. — (Destination solar system)
    Includes index.
    ISBN 978-1-4358-3449-1 (lib. bdg.) — ISBN 978-1-4358-3469-9 (pbk.) —
ISBN 978-1-4358-3470-5 (6-pack)
    1. Meteors—Juvenile literature. 2. Asteroids—Juvenile literature.
3. Comets—Juvenile literature. I. Title.
    QB741.5.S637 2010
    523.44—dc22

                                        2009002620

Manufactured in China

CONTENTS

>>>>>>> >>>>>>>

SPACE ROCKS

The space between the planets of our **solar system** is not empty. It is full of **billions** of objects, ranging in size from specks of dust to balls of rock hundreds of miles (km) across.

There are three main types of space rocks: asteroids, comets, and meteoroids. Asteroids are odd-shaped lumps of rock not large enough to be called planets. The largest, Ceres, is 578 miles (930 km) across, but most asteroids are much smaller. There are thousands that are a few miles (km) wide and billions the size of large stones.

Comets are chunks of dusty ice that orbit the Sun on the edge of the solar system. The only ones we get to see from Earth are the few that swoop past our planet from time to time. These travel around the Sun in very stretched **orbits**, taking them close to the Sun at one point and then far away again. As comets approach the Sun, **radiation** heats them up and they grow a bright tail.

This diagram of the solar system shows the asteroid belt (blue), the orbit of a near-Earth asteroid (red), and the stretched orbit of a comet (green).

Specks of dust and chunks of rock moving through space are meteoroids. Meteoroids that enter Earth's **atmosphere** usually burn up in the sky. These are called meteors or shooting stars. Large meteoroids that pass through the atmosphere and hit the ground are called meteorites.

Space rocks often pass very close to Earth. Our planet gets hit by large ones every few million years.

Comets that pass close to Earth are some of the brightest objects in the sky. Some of them are even visible during the day.

INTO THE ASTEROID BELT

Your **mission** will take you away from Earth and through the **asteroid belt** and then back home again alongside a comet.

ROCKY REGION

The asteroid belt is about 250 million miles (400 million km) from the Sun. The journey from Earth takes eight months, and after a **flyby** of Mars, you are finally approaching the belt's inner edge.

The rocks look crowded together on your map of the belt, but the large asteroids are actually so far apart that you can rarely see more than one at a time. Nevertheless, occasional collisions send chunks of rock spinning off in unexpected directions, so you need to be on the lookout.

The asteroid belt has 10 billion lumps of rock in it.

LIGHT AND DARK

Many of the asteroids you see look different from each other. Some are brown, some are red, and others glint like metal. However, most are pitch-black and only show up on your **radar**.

You are heading for giant Ceres. This is one of the few asteroids that has enough **gravity** to pull itself into a ball shape. Smaller asteroids have irregular forms.

SMASHED TO PIECES

A couple of times you almost crash into a cloud of rubble. It is the remains of larger asteroids that were smashed in a collision. When asteroids collide, they split apart, and the pieces slowly spread out around the asteroid belt.

ASTEROID GROUPS

Most asteroids are in a belt, which lies between the orbits of Mars and Jupiter. This belt has several gaps in it, where it has been swept clear by Jupiter's gravity. There are also separate clusters of asteroids, called the Trojans, within Jupiter's orbit. Near-Earth asteroids (NEAs), such as the Apollos, Atens, and Amors, orbit nearer to the Sun in paths that come close to Earth's orbit.

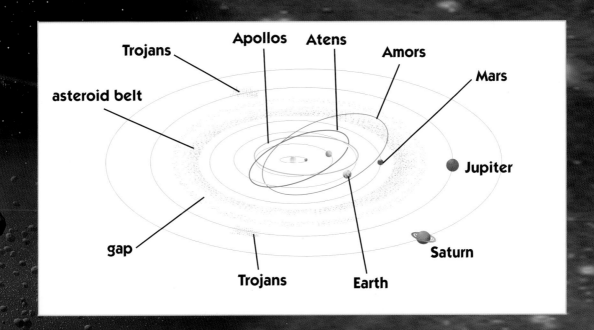

Trojans · Apollos · Atens · Amors · Mars · asteroid belt · Jupiter · gap · Trojans · Earth · Saturn

LEFTOVERS

You begin to wonder why the asteroids are different from each other. **Astronomers** think most asteroids are the remains of smashed planets. In the solar system's early days, chunks of rock bumped into each other and stuck together. They gradually formed **planetesimals**—rocky balls the size of Ceres.

Many asteroids have glassy lumps called chondrules in them, which formed at the very start of the solar system.

HEAT EFFECT

Some planetesimals were heated up by all the collisions and melted inside. Heavy metals, such as iron, sunk toward the center, while lighter, rocky crystals floated at the surface.

GIANT NEIGHBOR

As nearby Jupiter began to grow, its gravity disturbed the orbits of the planetesimals in the area, making them smash into each other harder and more frequently. As a result, the planetesimals broke up again. Some asteroids are chunks of iron from the centers of the planetesimals, while others formed from the rocky surface layers.

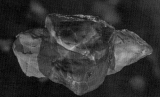

SMALL WORLDS

On the way to Ceres, you see some **amazing** sights. Some asteroids have their own tiny moons, while others orbit around each other in pairs. Then, Ceres comes into view. It is enormous!

In 2006, Ceres was made a dwarf planet along with Pluto and Eris. This single asteroid weighs half as much as all the other asteroids put together!

ROCK BALL

Ceres looks like a tiny version of Earth's Moon. You can see many little **craters**. The asteroid has very low gravity to pull your spaceship into orbit, so you have to slow down and steer carefully.

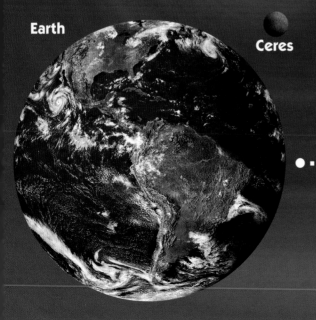

Earth

Ceres

TINY WORLD

Landing is also hard, you could easily overshoot. On the surface, you are very light. You take a leap into the sky and do not come down for more than a minute! The horizon is much closer than you are used to. You can see the curve of Ceres clearly.

Your instrument pack tells you that Ceres's dark surface is rich in chemicals with carbon in them—the same **element** in soot and pencil leads. The rocks also have ice and water trapped inside them.

Although Ceres is the largest asteroid, it is tiny in comparison to Earth, as this artist's impression shows. Earth is about 13 times wider than Ceres.

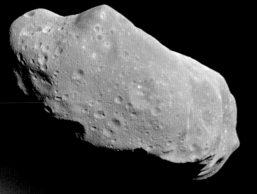

LIGHT ROCK

Next you travel to Mathilde, an asteroid about 35 miles (55 km) across. Mathilde's gravity seems weak even for its small size. Your sensors show that the asteroid is only slightly **denser** than water. Mathilde must have caverns inside it. Perhaps it was made from a jumble of rocks jammed together with gaps in between.

Astronomers think that Hektor, the largest Trojan asteroid, might actually be two rocks that spin around each other very closely.

NEAR TO EARTH

Your final stop is Eros, a **near-Earth asteroid** (NEA) about the size of Manhattan Island in New York. Eros orbits outside of the main belt, between Mars and Earth. Its surface is paler than other asteroids. It is made from silica, the **mineral** found in sand. Eros has a narrow middle and bulges at both ends. The strange shape does odd things to its gravity. The pull of gravity is stronger on the bulges than in the middle. Pebbles knocked by your feet roll uphill as you walk!

10

LOOKING AT ASTEROIDS

Asteroids are so small that they were only discovered after astronomers started using telescopes.

A German scientist named Karl Gauss used math to figure out that Ceres went around the Sun.

NEW PLANET?

The discovery of the first asteroid, Ceres, was an accident. Ceres was first seen by the Italian astronomer Giuseppe Piazzi in 1801. Piazzi was mapping the stars when he noticed that one faint object had moved.

Piazzi thought he had found a new planet and named it Ceres, after the Roman goddess of farming. However, other astronomers thought that Ceres was too faint to be a planet, and many kept looking for one. Soon more objects—Pallas, Juno, and Vesta—were discovered.

Over the next 20 years, hundreds more objects were discovered. British astronomer William Herschel named them asteroids, which means "starlike objects."

Even today, asteroids are discovered by accident. These streaks of light are unknown asteroids showing up on photos taken with a space telescope.

Asteroids are the only objects in space that are named by their discoverers.

The first ones were named after ancient Greek and Roman gods and goddesses.

Four asteroids are named John, Paul, George, and Ringo, after the Beatles.

Asteroid number 9007 is called James Bond, after the famous movie spy!

A view of Earth from Toutatis, an asteroid that passes very close to Earth, just beyond the Moon, every four years.

GETTING INTERESTED

Most astronomers **ignored** asteroids. They were just something that blocked the view of more distant objects. That changed when they realized that NEAs might hit Earth one day. They also found that asteroids could teach them a lot about the early solar system.

CLOSER LOOKS

Space **probes** heading to the outer planets provided the first close-up views of asteroids. Then in 1996,

NASA sent *NEAR-Shoemaker*, the *Near Earth Asteroid Rendezvous* probe into space. It was the first probe made to study asteroids. It carried cameras, chemical detectors, and sensors looking for **magnetic fields** around asteroids. *NEAR-Shoemaker* made flybys of Eros and Mathilde.

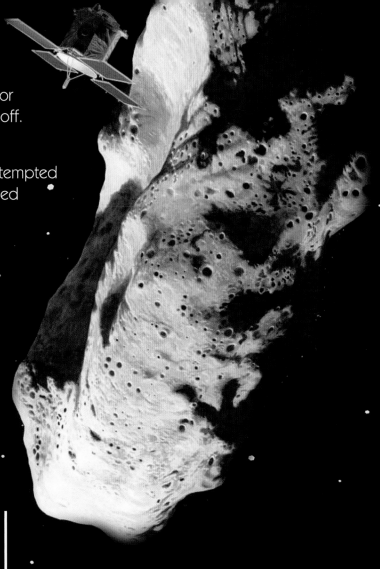

ASTEROID LANDER

The probe then went into orbit around Eros in 2000. After a year in orbit, *NEAR* then landed on Eros. The probe sent back data from the surface for more than two weeks before switching off.

DUST COLLECTOR

In 2005, *MUSES-C*, a Japanese probe attempted to collect a **sample** of another NEA called Itokawa. However, the probe missed! Astronomers think it did collect some dust from around the asteroid, which they will study when the probe comes back to Earth in 2010.

Astronomers expect to find a lot of metal in the dust. It might be possible in the **future** to mine asteroids. Just one could provide billions of dollars worth of iron, nickel, cobalt, and precious metals such as platinum.

NEAR-Shoemaker landed on the saddle-shaped dip in the middle of the asteroid.

RIDING WITH A COMET

It is time to leave the asteroids and head back to Earth. A large comet heading toward Earth and the Sun will soon pass close to you. Perhaps you can hitch a ride.

Comets are thought to be the remains of ice blocks that were thrown to the edge of the solar system billions of years ago.

QUIET COMET

When the comet comes into view, it is a letdown. You were expecting to see a glowing white ball with a magnificent tail, but all you see is a black stone tumbling slowly through space.

WHERE'S THE TAIL?

Comets travel along stretched orbits. This one's orbit is so **elliptical** that it appears to be heading directly toward the Sun. You steer your ship into orbit around the comet. It is about 6 miles (10 km) wide, and the dark surface is pitted with **impact** craters. How is this going to turn into a ball of light with a blazing tail? Perhaps the surface will offer some clues.

Comets are often described as "dirty snowballs" since they are made of ice, dust, and rock. | . . .●

DARK SURFACE

You land on the comet's dark side and take a walk in the gloom. Your weighted boots crunch on the loose ground, kicking up clouds of sooty dust. You dig down into the dust and soon find a paler **material**—ice.

BLAST FROM BENEATH

You then head over to the sunlit side of the comet, taking giant leaps toward the glowing horizon. The sunlight is stunning, but everywhere else is very dark. But then you spot another, fainter glow nearby. A jet of gas, dust, and ice is bursting out of the ground and glowing in the light. The comet is waking up.

FROZEN SOLID

You decide to head for a safe orbit around the comet before the surface gets too active. Now you have time to **analyze** the ice samples from the surface. The comet is mostly frozen water, but it also has frozen **carbon dioxide**, or dry ice, in it.

As the weeks pass, and the comet gets closer to the Sun, it gets more active. The sooty black lump you landed on—the comet's **nucleus**—is gradually warming up, and the ice underground is melting. However, liquid water cannot exist in the **vacuum** of space, so the ice then changes directly into water vapor. This gas bursts out of the nucleus in jets. Back in a safe orbit around the comet, you watch as new jets begin to erupt.

The sky outside the ship has become misty as more gas spews out of the nucleus. This growing ball of gas and ice grains is called the **coma**. Comet comas can grow to more than 100,000 miles (160,000 km) wide—eight times wider than Earth! Back on Earth, the comet will appear as a bright dot in the night sky.

SIDEWAYS VIEW

You decide to fly farther out for a better view and travel alongside the comet. As you cross the orbit of Mars, the comet's glowing tail begins to grow. Your instruments reveal that the tail is made from gas and dust from the coma that have been blown across space by the force of the Sun's energy.

This close-up view of Halley's Comet shows bright gas jets blasting out from one side of the comet.

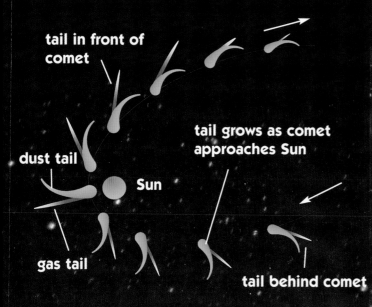

tail in front of comet

dust tail

Sun

gas tail

tail grows as comet approaches Sun

tail behind comet

Comets look as though they might be flying so fast that they form tails that stretch behind them, but that is not the case. They always point away from the Sun because of the force of the Sun's solar wind. The gas tail is straight, but the dust tail curves a little as it is affected more by the Sun's gravity.

TWO TAILS

From a distance you can see two tails: a narrow blue tail and a larger, yellowish white tail. The blue tail is made of gas blown from the coma by the **solar wind**. It glows blue because the solar wind makes the gas **atoms** give out light. The yellow tail is made of dust blown by the Sun's radiation, and it shines in reflected light.

DISTANT HOME

The comet you are traveling with has come a very long way. According to your calculations, it goes around the Sun once every half a million years!

The Oort Cloud is at the very edge of the solar system. A thicker section closer in is the Kuiper Belt, which surrounds the planets.

LONG JOURNEY

After your comet swoops close to the Sun, it will then fly back into the outer reaches of the solar system. What would you find if you could stay with it on its long journey into outer space?

LONG AND SHORT

Comets orbit the Sun in different planes from the planets. Long-period comets, such as Hale-Bopp, come from far out in the Oort Cloud on orbits that take thousands or millions of years. Short-period comets, such as Halley's Comet, visit the inner solar system much more frequently because their orbits are shorter.

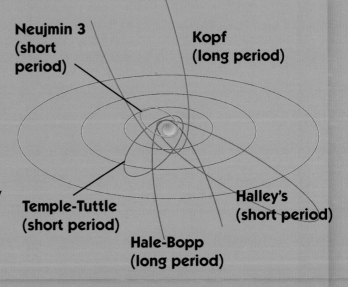

Neujmin 3 (short period)

Kopf (long period)

Temple-Tuttle (short period)

Hale-Bopp (long period)

Halley's (short period)

ON THE EDGE

Far beyond the planets lies the Oort Cloud. This cloud has several trillion cometlike bodies in it in a vast **sphere** around the solar system. The cloud is 100,000 times farther from the Sun than Earth.

FALLING IN

The Sun's gravity is so weak in the cloud that the bodies are easily disturbed by distant stars. When the ice is disturbed, a body may drift away into deep space or head toward the Sun and become a comet. Comets from the Oort Cloud take centuries to orbit the Sun.

CLOSE RELATIONS

Some comets orbit the Sun more quickly. These comets come from the Kuiper Belt, which spreads out beyond Neptune. Occasionally, Kuiper Belt objects are disturbed by Neptune's gravity and are sent plunging into the inner solar system as comets.

Astronomers think comets formed around 4.5 billion years ago, shortly after the solar system was born. Most of the material became the Sun and the planets, but comets came from ice that collected in the outer solar system. When larger planets formed, their gravity catapulted most of the comets out into space, forming the Oort Cloud. The ice left behind formed the Kuiper Belt.

The Kuiper Belt has several large bodies called dwarf planets. So far only two, Eris and Pluto, have been given a name.

UNDERSTANDING
COMETS

Comets have been seen throughout human history, but until 500 years ago people thought they were caused by the weather!

MYSTERIOUS LIGHTS

In 1577, the Danish astronomer Tycho Brahe showed that comets were traveling far out in space and were moving around the Sun, not Earth. However, comets were still very much a mystery. No one knew where comets came from or where they disappeared to.

DANGER APPROACHING!

Throughout history, people have seen comets as **omens** of disaster or great events. The arrival of a comet is always a big event, and their appearances have been recorded for hundreds of years.

An appearance of Halley's Comet is recorded in the Bayeux Tapestry, where it is shown as a sign of the coming Norman invasion of England in 1066.

Many of the comets
we know about were
discovered by
people looking
at the stars from
their backyards.

HALLEY'S SUCCESS

In 1705, the English
astronomer Edmond Halley
compiled a list of comets
based on observations
stretching back to the 1300s.
Halley noticed that three
sightings in 1531, 1607,
and 1682 had orbits that
were exactly the same. He
suggested they might be just
one comet with a 76-year
orbit. He was proved right
when the comet (named
Halley's Comet in his honor)
returned, as predicted, in
1758. Other returning comets
were soon identified, and
orbits for some of them
were calculated.

EDMOND HALLEY

**English
astronomer
Edmond Halley
is best known
for predicting
the return
of the comet
named after
him. However,
he made other
contributions
to science.
From 1676 to
1678, he traveled to the South
Atlantic and made the first accurate
maps of the southern skies, as well
as studying Earth's magnetism and
compiling charts to help sailors. In
1720, he became the second British
astronomer royal.**

ROBOT EXPLORERS

The nuclei of comets are hard to study from Earth because they are hidden deep inside their glowing comas. The only way to get a good look at a comet, therefore, is to send a space probe into the coma.

In 1985, **NASA** sent a probe called the *International Cometary Explorer* through the gas tail of Comet Giacobini-Zinner. The probe showed that the comet's nucleus was only about 1.6 miles (2.5 km) wide.

MEETING HALLEY

In 1986, five probes visited Halley's Comet during one of its regular visits. Two **Soviet**, two Japanese, and one European Space Agency (ESA) probe arrived at the comet during the same

week in March. The Soviet and Japanese probes flew within a few thousand miles (km) of the nucleus and photographed the coma.

The European probe, *Giotto*, plunged straight into the coma and took pictures of the nucleus through the misty cloud of gas and dust surrounding it. The probe revealed a dark, irregular lump of rock and ice about 10 miles (16 km) long and 5 miles (8 km) wide.

COMA SWEEP

NASA's *Stardust* probe flew close to Wild 2 in 2004. It collected samples of dust from the comet's coma and then carried it back to Earth. In 2006, the probe arrived home and parachuted a **lander** safely into the Utah desert.

Giotto **got within 370 miles (595 km) of the nucleus of Halley's Comet when it passed Earth in 1986.**

The *Deep Impact*
probe blasted
a hole in the
Tempel 1 comet.

MAKE A HOLE

In 2005, the *Deep Impact* probe was
sent to find out what was inside a
comet nucleus. The probe fired a
1,100-pound (500 kg) copper missile
into the comet Tempel 1 to create an
impact crater and find out what the
comet's inside is like.

The comet Shoemaker-Levy 9
broke up and crashed into Jupiter
in 1994. The impact churned up
bruises in Jupiter's atmosphere
that were larger than Earth itself.

SHOOTING STARS

You have now left the comet behind and returned to Earth, but even from here you can see signs of the many small objects that clutter our solar system.

STREAKS OF LIGHT

On a dark night, as you stare up into the starlit sky, a flash of movement catches your eye—a light zips across the sky before disappearing. You wait a few minutes and see another light, this time brighter and with a glowing yellow tail. These are shooting stars, or meteors.

HOT AND FAST

Meteors are tiny, ranging from the size of a sand grain to that of a pebble. They hit Earth's atmosphere at such great speeds, up to 165,000 miles per hour (266,000 km/h),

that they burn up in fireballs that are visible from the ground many miles (km) below. The larger the meteor, the longer it lasts and the bigger the fireball. Most meteors are gone in a flash, lasting less than a second.

LIGHT STORM

On most nights, there are about 10 shooting stars an hour, but tonight is different. Earth is moving through the trail of dust left by your comet, and shooting stars are appearing about once a minute. Astronomers call this a **meteor shower**.

METEOR SHOWERS

Meteor showers happen when Earth crosses the path of a comet (above). They happen at the same time each year and can be tied to certain comets. They are usually named for the constellation from which they appear to come, such as the Leonids (main picture), which come from the constellation Leo.

NAME	DATES	PARENT COMET
Eta Aquarids	May 1–10	Halley's Comet
Perseids	July 23–Aug 20	Comet Swift-Tuttle
Orionids	Oct 16–27	Halley's Comet
Leonids	Nov 15–20	Comet Tempel-Tuttle
Geminids	Dec 7–15	3200 Phaethon

IMPACT!

Occasionally a large chunk of rock makes it all the way to the ground. This is a meteorite.

ROCK FROM SPACE

As far as astronomers know, comets are ice, not rock, so where could meteorites come from? Asteroids are the most likely source because the two types of rock are made of similar materials.

Some meteorites may be pieces broken off NEAs by collisions, but astronomers think most have been swept out of the asteroid belt by Jupiter's gravity.

GLASSY DROPLETS

There are four types of meteorites. The first are chondrites. These have glassy **chondrules** in them. Scientists think chondrules formed as tiny droplets in the cloud of gas and dust that circled the Sun when the solar system was forming. In other words, chondrules are time capsules from before Earth existed. Ceres and Eros are made of chondrites.

MELTED ROCKS

Achondrite meteorites are made from chondrules that have melted together to form a single lump of rock. Achondrite rocks formed in the heart of large, hot asteroids.

This rock in Namibia is the largest meteorite ever discovered. It weighs 66 tons (60 t).

This tiny meteorite from Arizona is made of nickel and iron.

METAL AND STONE

Iron meteorites are lumps of metal, usually iron and nickel. They formed originally in the **cores** of planetesimals.

Stony-iron meteorites are the rarest meteorites of all. They consist of rock crystals embedded in metal, and they may have formed around the edge of planetesimal cores.

BIG HITTERS

Very rarely does a huge asteroid or comet hit Earth. Wind and rain have worn away most of the craters that were made, but large impacts occur every few centuries.

The Barringer Crater, in Arizona, is nearly 1 mile (1.6 km) wide. It was formed 50,000 years ago, by a 160-foot (50 m) wide meteorite.

DEADLY STRIKES

In 1908, a 1-million-ton (900,000 t) comet exploded above the Tunguska River in Siberia and flattened 770 square miles (2,000 sq km) of forest. This impact, known as the Tunguska Event, was visible more than 500 miles (800 km) away!

The most famous impact on Earth is the one thought to have helped kill the dinosaurs 65 million years ago.

Many astronomers think a comet 6 miles (10 km) wide struck the Gulf of Mexico around this time, creating a crater 186 miles (300 km) across. The **debris** thrown into the sky would have stayed in the atmosphere for years and blocked out sunlight. If a similar impact occurred today, most of the animals on Earth—including people—would be killed!

Astronomers watch the skies around Earth to make sure giant space rocks do not hit Earth without warning.

COULD HUMANS LIVE THERE?

L iving on asteroids or comets would be a major challenge.
But they might be a source of valuable minerals.

SPACE MINERS

Why would we want to send people to visit one of these small worlds? Asteroid mining could change space travel from expensive exploration into a business. Although the mining could probably be done by machines, astronauts might be needed to set up and repair equipment. Inexpensive raw materials supplied to factories in giant orbiting space stations could transform life on Earth.

A base on an asteroid would need to be supplied with water and fuel from Earth.

GLOSSARY

amazing (uh-MAYZ-ing) Wonderful.

analyze (A-nuh-lyz) To find out about something using scientific tests.

asteroid belt (AS-teh-royd BELT) The ring of asteroids that orbit the Sun between the orbits of Mars and Jupiter.

astronomers (uh-STRAH-nuh-merz) People who study the Sun, the Moon, the planets, and the stars.

atmosphere (AT-muh-sfeer) The layer of gas trapped by gravity around the surface of a planet.

atoms (A-temz) Minute pieces of matter.

billions (BIL-yunz) Thousands of millions.

carbon dioxide (KAR-bin dy-OK-syd) A heavy colorless gas.

chondrules (KON-droolz) Small spheres of mineral inside an asteroid or meteor, formed when molten rock cooled billions of years ago.

coma (KOH-muh) The cloud of gas that grows around the nucleus of a comet as it gets close to the Sun.

cores (KORZ) Centers of planets, stars, or moons.

craters (KRAY-turz) Circular holes made when comets, asteroids, or meteorites hit a planet or moon.

debris (duh-BREE) Pieces of rock, dust, ice, or other materials.

denser (DENTS-er) Having more weight squeezed into a space than something else.

element (EH-luh-ment) A chemical that cannot be split into any other chemicals.

elliptical (ih-LIP-tih-kul) Having an oval shape.

flyby (FLY-by) A mission in which a space probe passes close to a planet but is traveling too fast to go into orbit around the planet.

future (FYOO-chur) The time that is coming.

gravity (GRA-vih-tee) The force that pulls objects together. The heavier or closer an object is, the stronger its gravity, or pull.

ignored (ig-NORD) Paid no attention to something.

impact (IM-pakt) When two objects hit each other.

lander (LAN-der) A spacecraft that lands on a planet, moon, or asteroid.

magnetic fields (mag-NEH-tik FEELDZ) Regions around objects where a compass can detect the object's north pole.

material (muh-TEER-ee-ul) What something is made of.

meteor shower (MEE-tee-or SHOW-er) When hundreds of shooting stars burn up in a planet's atmosphere in a few hours.

mineral (MIN-rul) A type of solid chemical found in rock.

mission (MIH-shun) An expedition to visit a certain place in space, such as a planet, moon, or comet.

NASA (NA-suh) The National Aeronautics and Space Administration, the U.S. space agency in charge of sending people and probes into space.

near-Earth asteroid (NEA) (NIR-erth AS-teh-royd) An asteroid with an orbit that brings it close to Earth.

nucleus (NOO-klee-us) The solid lump of ice in the center of a comet.

omens (OH-menz) Predictions of the future.

orbits (OR-bits) Paths objects take around others when they are trapped by the heavier object's gravity.

planetesimals (pla-neh-TEH-suh-mulz) Small, planetlike balls of debris that formed in the early solar system.

probes (PROHBZ) Robotic vehicles sent from Earth to study the solar system.

radar (RAY-dahr) Technology that uses radio waves to calculate an object's position or shape.

radiation (ray-dee-AY-shun) Energy let out in rays from a source. Heat and light are types of radiation.

sample (SAM-pul) A small part of something, given to show what the rest of it is like.

solar system (SOH-ler SIS-tem) The planets, asteroids, and comets that orbit the Sun.

solar wind (SOH-ler WIND) A stream of electrified gas that flies out of the Sun and across space at very a high speed.

Soviet (SOH-vee-et) Having to do with the Soviet Union, an empire centered on Russia that ruled a huge area, stretching from Europe to East Asia, in the twentieth century.

sphere (SFEER) An object that is shaped like a ball.

vacuum (VA-kyoom) Space where no matter exists.

INDEX

WEB SITES

Due to the changing nature of Internet links, PowerKids Press has developed an online list of Web sites related to the subject of this book. This site is updated regularly. Please use this link to access the list:
www.powerkidslinks.com/dsol/astcom/